Cornerstones of Freedom

The Louisiana Purchase

Gail Sakurai

CHILDREN'S PRESS®
A Division of Grolier Publishing
New York • London • Hong Kong • Sydney
Danbury, Connecticut

Library of Congress Cataloging-in-Publication Data

Sakurai, Gail.
  The Louisiana Purchase / Gail Sakurai.
    p. cm.—(Cornerstones of freedom)
  Includes index.
  Summary: Chronicles the historical background and political
maneuvers that led to the Louisiana Purchase by President Thomas
Jefferson in 1803.
  ISBN 0-516-20791-1 (lib. bdg.)   0-516-26336-6 (pbk.)
  1. Louisiana Purchase—Juvenile literature. [1. Louisiana
Purchase.] I. Title. II. Series.
E333.S25   1998
973.4'6—dc21
                                      97-12015
                                          CIP
                                          AC

On April 9, 1682, a group of French explorers stood on the banks of the Mississippi River. They had just completed a three-month journey down the great waterway to its mouth in the Gulf of Mexico. They were the first Europeans to see the huge delta where the Mississippi River ended. The travelers watched as their leader, René Robert Cavelier, Sieur de La Salle, erected a cross and a wooden column on which was painted the French coat of arms. Then, La Salle solemnly read from a document that claimed the Mississippi River and all of its lands for France. La Salle named the territory "Louisiana" in honor of the French king, Louis XIV.

René Robert Cavelier, Sieur de La Salle

As his companions and an audience of American Indians watch, La Salle claims the Mississippi River basin for France.

A year after its founding in 1718, the city of New Orleans was little more than a collection of houses on the banks of the Mississippi River.

Spanish conquistadors had explored the Mississippi region more than a hundred years before La Salle, but Spain had not established colonies in the area. Instead, the Spanish had turned their attention south, to the gold-rich lands of Mexico and Peru. Unlike the Spanish, the French quickly settled in Louisiana and solidified their claim to the territory. In 1718, France founded the town of New Orleans 100 miles (160 kilometers) above the mouth of the Mississippi River. Four years later, New Orleans became the capital of Louisiana.

From 1754 to 1763, France waged a bitter struggle with Great Britain for control of the North American continent. By 1763, France had been defeated, losing most of its territory in North America. All of France's land west of the Mississippi River, as well as the city of New Orleans, passed to Spain. Great Britain took possession of Canada and all the land east of the Mississippi River.

Then, in 1776, the thirteen English colonies in North America declared their independence from Great Britain and became the United States of America. When the American Revolution finally ended in 1783, Great Britain agreed to give the land between the Mississippi and the Appalachian Mountains to the United States. Immediately, Americans began pouring across the mountains and settling the new territory.

For Americans in 1792, the "West" was the unsettled area of land between the original thirteen states and the Mississippi River.

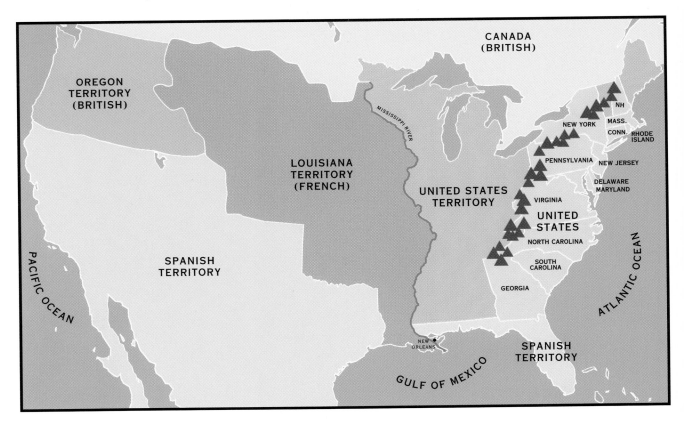

There were no major roads to connect the western territory to large cities on the Atlantic Ocean. Fur traders in the western wilderness and farmers in Kentucky and Tennessee had to float their goods down the Mississippi River to New Orleans. Then the goods were shipped from New Orleans to the East Coast of the

United States or to Europe. The Mississippi River became an important highway for trade and commerce, and New Orleans was a major port on the great waterway.

Spain allowed United States citizens free access to the Mississippi River and the "right of deposit" at New Orleans. This meant that Americans could ship their goods down the river and through New Orleans without having to pay any duties or taxes to Spanish authorities. A tax at New Orleans would seriously cripple American trade.

By the 1800s, the Mississippi River was a heavily traveled trading route.

In March 1801, Thomas Jefferson became the third president of the United States. Jefferson was a man of many talents and interests. He was a statesman, writer, scientist, inventor, architect, and farmer. Jefferson had wide

President Jefferson, a man of many talents, dreamed that the United States would one day stretch all the way to the Pacific Ocean.

experience in government, having served as governor of Virginia, secretary of state, minister to France, and vice president of the United States. He was the author of the Declaration of Independence and had written a well-known book about Virginia and its wilderness areas beyond the Appalachian Mountains.

Although he was the owner of a large plantation in Charlottesville, Virginia, Thomas Jefferson considered himself a simple farmer. He was sympathetic to the interests of the settlers in the western lands, and he supported exploration of the wilderness and westward expansion of the United States. Jefferson even dreamed of a great nation that would one day stretch all the way to the Pacific Ocean. He said, "It is impossible not to look forward to distant times, when our [nation] will cover the whole northern, if not the southern continent, with a people speaking the same language, governed in similar forms, and by similar laws."

Shortly after Jefferson became president, disturbing rumors began circulating of a secret agreement between France and Spain. The rumors claimed that Spain had given the territories of Louisiana, New Orleans, and East and West Florida to France.

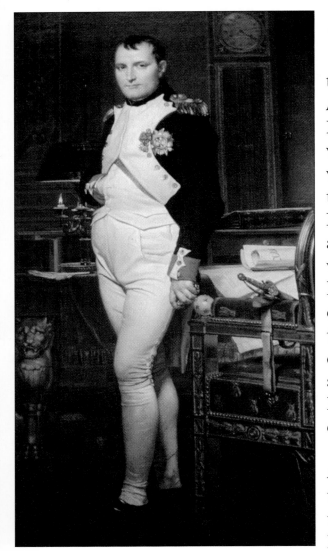

Napoleon, a powerful and ambitious leader, had won many spectacular military victories in Europe.

Spain was a weak country that posed little threat to American interests. But President Jefferson was worried about France. France was a powerful nation, and the French leader, Napoleon Bonaparte, was ambitious and aggressive. Bonaparte was a military genius who had already conquered much of Europe, and he hoped to establish a vast French empire in North America. A strong French presence in Louisiana could be a great danger to the United States.

Robert Livingston, the American minister to France, tried to determine whether the rumors were true. But the French leaders ignored his questions. "The [French] Minister will give no answer," Livingston complained. "He will not say what their boundaries are, what are their intentions, and when they are to take possession."

Finally, in 1802, the United States discovered that the rumors concerning Spain and France were indeed true. The two countries had already signed a secret treaty on October 1, 1800. Spain

Robert Livingston, American minister to France, had the difficult task of negotiating with the French government.

had agreed to give the Louisiana Territory to France in return for Tuscany, a valuable region of Italy. But no American knew exactly how much North American land was involved. The treaty stated only that Spain ceded to France "the colony or province of Louisiana with the same extent it now has in the hands of Spain, and that it had when France possessed it."

At the very least, the treaty gave France control of New Orleans and all the land west of the Mississippi River to the Rocky Mountains. It was not clear, however, whether the important Spanish territories of East and West Florida, which bordered the Gulf of Mexico, were included in the transfer.

The American settlers and traders in the western regions of the United States needed a river outlet and a port on the Gulf of Mexico. The Floridas had many large rivers that flowed to the Gulf. James Madison, the U.S. secretary of state, declared that the free use of these rivers was extremely important to the United States. President Jefferson instructed Robert Livingston

James Madison claimed that the rivers to the Gulf of Mexico were essential to the survival of the United States.

to try to buy New Orleans and East and West Florida from the French. If the French would not agree to sell those lands, at the very least the United States needed a guarantee of free passage down the Mississippi River and trading rights at the port of New Orleans.

For weeks, Livingston tried to persuade the French to sell New Orleans and the Floridas to the United States, but his efforts were unsuccessful. "There never was a government in which less could be done by negotiation than here," Livingston exploded in frustration.

France had not yet sent someone to take control of Louisiana, so Spanish officials in New Orleans continued to govern. Then, on October 15, 1802, the Spanish canceled the U.S. right of deposit at New Orleans. Americans could still use the Mississippi River and trade their goods in New Orleans, but they would have to pay duties and port fees, just like other foreigners.

Western Americans were outraged. They regarded free access to the Mississippi and New Orleans as their natural right. In their minds, being charged taxes was the same as being denied use of the river and the port. They protested loudly and demanded that President Jefferson and the Congress do something to protect their rights. If the U.S. government didn't act promptly, the frontiersmen might take

Spain demanded that all American goods exiting the Mississippi River at New Orleans be taxed.

matters into their own hands. There was wild talk of arming themselves and launching an expedition down the Mississippi to capture New Orleans. Americans in the East Coast states were also concerned about events in New Orleans because they needed the goods that the westerners shipped through that port city.

In January 1803, Jefferson decided to send James Monroe to Paris to assist Robert Livingston with the negotiations for New Orleans and the Floridas. Monroe was a former governor of Virginia and a former minister to France. He was also known as a friend of the

James Monroe was sent to Paris to help Livingston negotiate for Louisiana.

western Americans, and his appointment would reassure them that their interests were being looked after. Jefferson informed Monroe, "All eyes, all hopes, are now fixed on you."

Congress voted to pay two million dollars for the purchase of New Orleans and East and West Florida. But Jefferson privately authorized Monroe and Livingston to go as high as ten million dollars. James Monroe sailed for France on March 8, 1803.

Meanwhile, war was looming between France and Great Britain. Bonaparte was determined to conquer Great Britain and add it to his European empire. Great Britain was equally determined to defeat Bonaparte. The French ruler began making preparations to invade Great Britain, but he needed money to supply his invasion force. He also worried that the United States or England might try to seize his North American colonies once war started in Europe. Bonaparte had heard rumors that fifty thousand American frontiersmen were armed and ready to take New Orleans by force. U.S. newspapers confirmed the reports of war fever in the American West.

Napoleon Bonaparte decided to sell all of Louisiana to the United States to raise the funds he needed for an invasion of Great Britain. Bonaparte would use the money to buy guns and ammunition. Once he had conquered England, he would turn his attention to recovering his empire in North America. Bonaparte told his advisors about his decision, "I already consider the colony as entirely lost. It is not only New Orleans that I will cede, it is the whole colony without any reservations. . . . To attempt to retain it would be folly."

Special envoy James Monroe arrived in Paris on April 12, 1803. Robert Livingston quickly

informed Monroe that negotiations with the French had proved useless. "Only force can give us New Orleans," he said. "We must employ force. Let us first get possession of the country and negotiate afterwards."

Surrounded by his closest advisors, Napoleon discusses the possibility of selling the Louisiana Territory to the United States.

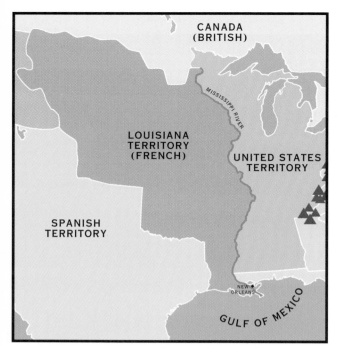

Monroe and Livingston were shocked when France offered the entire Louisiana Territory for sale.

The following evening, while Monroe and Livingston were eating dinner, they received a visit from François Barbé-Marbois, the French minister of the treasury. Livingston and Monroe were astounded when Barbé-Marbois informed them of Bonaparte's willingness to sell the entire territory of Louisiana. The two Americans knew it was an opportunity too good to pass up. However, there were problems.

Livingston and Monroe were supposed to negotiate for New Orleans and East and West Florida. They weren't authorized to purchase the entire Louisiana Territory. They considered sending a message to Jefferson and waiting for new instructions. But it would take many weeks for messages to travel back and forth across the Atlantic Ocean, and Bonaparte was anxious to conclude the deal. He needed funds for the coming war with Great Britain. He threatened to withdraw the offer if the Americans didn't act immediately.

In addition, the Americans didn't know the exact boundaries of the territory they were buying. Louisiana was generally agreed to extend from the Mississippi River west to the Rocky Mountains, and from the Gulf of Mexico in the

Monroe and Livingston (standing) negotiate with a French official.

south to Canada in the north. But Livingston and Monroe weren't sure if East or West Florida were included in the agreement, and the French wouldn't give them a straight answer on that point. The French also failed to inform the Americans that Bonaparte had promised the Spanish king that he would not cede Louisiana to any country other than Spain. In spite of the confusing details, the Americans decided to go ahead with the purchase. Livingston explained, "I was willing to take it [Louisiana] in any form."

Livingston and Monroe were authorized to spend only ten million dollars; the French were asking more than seventeen million. For several days the Americans bargained over the price of Louisiana. Livingston wrote to Secretary of State Madison, "We shall do all we can to cheapen the purchase, but my present sentiment is that we shall buy." In the end, the two countries agreed on fifteen million dollars. The U.S. government had to borrow money for the purchase from English and Dutch banks.

Livingston and Monroe sign the treaty.

The treaty that gave all the details of the purchase agreement was dated April 30, 1803. At the signing ceremony, Livingston said, "This is the noblest work of our whole lives. From this day the United States take their place among the powers of first rank." The Americans had just purchased 827,987 square miles (2,144,485 square kilometers) of land, at the price of about four cents an acre.

The treaty arrived in Washington, D.C., on July 14, 1803. Both President Jefferson and the Congress had to officially approve it. Although Jefferson was anxious to acquire the vast Louisiana Territory for the United States, he was worried about the legality of the agreement.

Jefferson believed that the United States Constitution granted the national government only limited powers. All other authority belonged to the individual states. The Constitution did not state that the national government could buy foreign lands. However, the Constitution did provide for the making of treaties with other countries. Jefferson reasoned that the Louisiana Purchase was a treaty, and therefore it did not violate the spirit of the Constitution. Jefferson later admitted that he had "stretched the Constitution until it cracked."

Some members of Congress were also worried about violating the Constitution. Other congressmen were opposed to the purchase because they feared that the influence and power of the eastern states would decrease as a result. Nevertheless, the majority in Congress, as well as the majority of the American public, was overwhelmingly in favor of purchasing Louisiana. The United States Senate ratified the treaty on October 20, 1803, by a vote of 27 to 7.

The Louisiana Purchase Treaty— Thomas Jefferson's signature appears on the left page above the eagle stamp

The same day, the House of Representatives authorized borrowing the money to pay for the Louisiana Territory by a vote of 89 to 23.

The Spanish were furious when they learned of the sale. They complained that the United States had no right to Louisiana, because France had promised never to transfer the territory to any other country. The Americans replied that this was not their concern. President Jefferson declared that "[Spain's complaints] were private questions between France and Spain which they must solve together." There was little Spain could do against the strength of France and the determination of the United States, but the

Spanish wanted to make it clear to the Americans that East and West Florida were not part of the sale. The Floridas were separate from Louisiana, and they still belonged to Spain.

Spain finally stopped protesting and formally transferred Louisiana to France on November 30, 1803, in a ceremony at New Orleans. Twenty days later, the United States received Louisiana from France. The American flag was raised over New Orleans for the first time on December 20, 1803.

Joyful citizens watch as the American flag is raised above New Orleans.

In 1804, Congress divided the huge territory to make it easier to govern. The southern part, covering roughly the same area as the present-day state of Louisiana, became the Territory of Orleans. The much larger northern area became the District of Louisiana. A year later, it was renamed the Territory of Louisiana.

President Jefferson had long hoped to send an expedition to explore and map the western wilderness. The Louisiana Territory was still largely unknown and uncharted by the United States, and it seemed wise to discover the size and nature of this new property.

Jefferson appointed his personal secretary, Meriwether Lewis, and Lewis's friend, William Clark, to lead the expedition. Both men had military and wilderness experience and shared

Meriwether Lewis and William Clark

Jefferson's interest in exploration. Lewis and Clark were instructed to draw maps, record scientific observations, and collect specimens of plants, animals, and minerals. Most importantly, Lewis and Clark were to find a water route to the Pacific Ocean.

A page from William Clark's journal shows his drawing of a bass fish.

People had dreamed for centuries of a shortcut across the North American continent that would make trade with China and other Asian countries much easier. With such a water route, ships would not have to spend two or three years sailing around South America to China and back.

Lewis and Clark experienced several adventures while traveling through the Louisiana Territory.

The Lewis and Clark expedition left St. Louis, a small trading post on the Mississippi River, on May 14, 1804. The explorers followed a branch of the Mississippi River, called the Missouri River, west. They crossed the Rocky Mountains on horseback and eventually paddled down the Columbia River to the Pacific Ocean. They finally arrived back in St. Louis on September 23, 1806, having traveled a total of 8,000 miles (12,870 kilometers). Lewis and Clark brought back hundreds of scientific specimens, numerous maps, and notes on the climate, soil, plants, and animals of the West. They did not find a water route to the Pacific, but their explorations showed that such a

This map details Lewis and Clark's journey west.

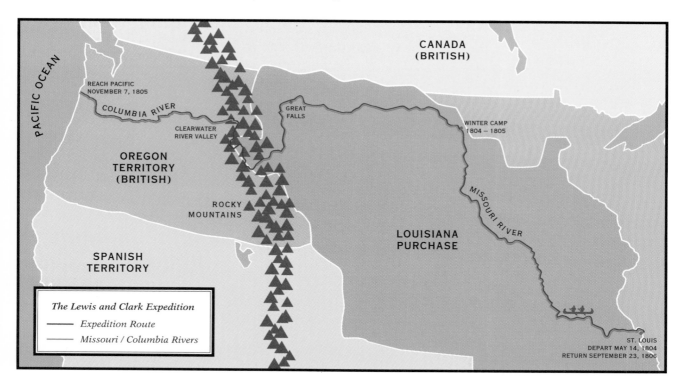

PACIFIC OCEAN

CANADA
(BRITISH)

REACH PACIFIC
NOVEMBER 7, 1805

COLUMBIA RIVER

GREAT
FALLS

WINTER CAMP
1804 – 1805

CLEARWATER
RIVER VALLEY

OREGON
TERRITORY
(BRITISH)

ROCKY
MOUNTAINS

MISSOURI RIVER

LOUISIANA
PURCHASE

SPANISH
TERRITORY

The Lewis and Clark Expedition
—— *Expedition Route*
—— *Missouri / Columbia Rivers*

ST. LOUIS
DEPART MAY 14, 1804
RETURN SEPTEMBER 23, 1806

passageway did not exist. The expedition was considered a tremendous success. As a reward, Meriwether Lewis was appointed governor of the Louisiana Territory, and William Clark became the Territory's superintendent of Indian affairs.

Disputes with Spain over the exact boundaries of the Louisiana Purchase continued for many years. Spain insisted that East and West Florida had never been part of the transfer to France and were still Spanish property. In 1819, Spain finally agreed to give the Floridas to the United States.

The Louisiana Purchase gave the United States valuable new land and doubled the young country's size. "The acquisition is great and glorious in itself; but still greater and more glorious are the means by

With the Louisiana Territory now part of the United States, the North American continent was opened to American settlers.

which it is obtained," proclaimed a leading newspaper, the *National Intelligencer*, in January 1804. Never in history, the newspaper boasted, had so much land been exchanged so peacefully. Above all, the Louisiana Purchase opened the way for westward expansion and the realization of Thomas Jefferson's vision of a great nation that stretched from the Atlantic to the Pacific.

The land from the Louisiana Purchase would later become several states.

THE LOUISIANA TERRITORY

It took more than one hundred years to finally settle the Louisiana Territory and divide it into thirteen states. Here is a list of the states and the dates they entered the Union:

State	Date Admitted
Louisiana (18th state)	1812
Missouri (24th state)	1821
Arkansas (25th state)	1836
Iowa (29th state)	1846
Minnesota (32nd state)	1858
Kansas (34th state)	1861
Nebraska (37th state)	1867
Colorado (38th state)	1876
North Dakota (39th state)	1889
South Dakota (40th state)	1889
Montana (41st state)	1889
Wyoming (44th state)	1890
Oklahoma (46th state)	1907

GLOSSARY

coat of arms – a design on a shield that serves as the emblem for a family or country

colony – a territory that is far away from the country that governs it

delta – a triangle-shaped area of land at the mouth of a river

duty – a tax paid on goods brought into or taken out of a country

empire – a group of countries under one government or ruler

envoy

envoy – a government official who is sent on a special diplomatic mission

expedition – a journey undertaken by a group of people with a specific purpose

minister – a person who is in charge of a department of the government

treaty

port – a city with a harbor where ships can anchor

ratify – to formally approve or confirm

treaty – a formal agreement or pact between countries

TIMELINE

1541 Spanish explorers reach the Mississippi River

1682 La Salle claims Louisiana for France

City of New Orleans founded **1718**

French and Indian War { **1754**
1762 France gives Louisiana to Spain
1763

American Revolution { **1775**
1783

Spain gives Louisiana back to France **1800**

1803

1804 } Lewis and Clark explore the
1806 } Louisiana Territory

1812 Louisiana becomes the eighteenth state

1819 The United States acquires East and West Florida from Spain

The United States purchases Louisiana from France

INDEX (*Boldface* page numbers indicate illustrations.)

PHOTO CREDITS

Photographs ©: National Portrait Gallery, Smithsonian Institution/Art Resource, NY: 15, 30 top; National Portrait Gallery, Smithsonian Institution; gift of the Regents of the Smithsonian Institution, the Thomas Jefferson Memorial Foundation, and the Enid and Crosby Kemper Foundation; owned jointly with Monticello/Art Resource, NY: 1, 8; Brown Brothers: 4, 6, 31 top; Corbis-Bettmann: 10, 11, 19; Culver Pictures: cover, 23; Erich Lessing/Art Resource, NY: 22, 30 bottom; Giraudon/Art Resource, NY: 2; Courtesy Historic New Orleans Collection: 17, 20, 31 bottom left; Courtesy of Montana Historical Society: 25 bottom, 31 right; North Wind Picture Archives: 3, 7, 12, 13, 14, 24, 25 top, 27; PhotoDisc, Inc.: 28, 29.

ABOUT THE AUTHOR

Gail Sakurai is a children's author who specializes in retelling folk tales and writing nonfiction for young readers. She is a full member of the Society of Children's Book Writers and Illustrators. For the Cornerstone of Freedom series, she has written *The Liberty Bell, Paul Revere,* and *The Jamestown Colony. The Louisiana Purchase* is her seventh book.

Ms. Sakurai lives in Cincinnati, Ohio, with her husband and two sons. When she is not researching or writing, she enjoys traveling with her family and visiting America's historical sites.